D1489321

POSTCARDS · FROM ·

The West Indies

Helen Arnold

RSVP

RAINTREE STECK-VAUGHN

P U B L I S H E R S

The Steck-Vaughn Company

Austin, Texas

Published by Raintree Steck-Vaughn Publishers, an imprint of Steck-Vaughn Company

A ZOË BOOK

Editors: Kath Davies, Pam Wells
Design: Sterling Associates
Map: Julian Baker
Production: Grahame Griffiths

Library of Congress Cataloging-in-Publication Data

Arnold, Helen.
    The West Indies / Helen Arnold.
        p. cm. — (Postcards from)
    "A Zoë Book" T.p. verso.
    Includes index.
    Summary: A collection of fictional postcards, written as if by young people visiting the West Indies, describes various sights and life in the islands.
    ISBN 0-8172-4021-7 (hardcover). — ISBN 0-8172-6204-0 (softcover)
    1. The West Indies—Juvenile literature. 2. Postcards—West Indies—Juvenile Literature. [1. West Indies—Description and travel. 2. Postcards.]
I. Title. II. Series.
F1608.3. A76 1997
972.9—dc20   96–3497
                                                                  CIP
                                                                   AC
Printed and bound in the United States
1 2 3 4 5 6 7 8 9 0 WZ 99 98 97 96

Photographic acknowledgments

The publishers wish to acknowledge, with thanks, the following photographic sources:

FLPA / K Aitken - cover bl; / Hans Dieter Brandl 18; Larsen Collinge - cover r; / Louise Murray 6; / Fred Friberg 10; / Robert Harding 16; / Robert Harding Picture Library; The Hutchison Library / Nancy Durrell McKenna 24; / Philip Wolmuth 26; South American Pictures / Rolando Pujol - title page, 14; Zefa - cover tl, 8, 12, 20, 22.

The publishers have made every effort to trace the copyright holders, but if they have inadvertently overlooked any, they will be pleased to make the necessary arrangement at the first opportunity.

Contents

All the words that appear in **bold** are explained in the Glossary on page 30.

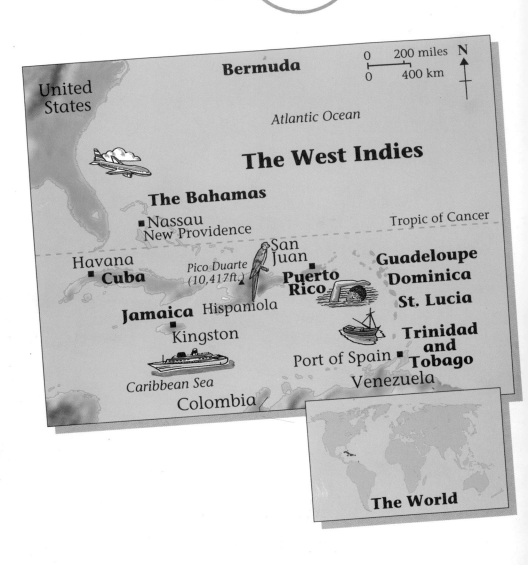

The following place names appear on the map:

Bermuda

United States

Atlantic Ocean

The West Indies

0   200 miles   N
0   400 km

The Bahamas

Nassau
New Providence

Tropic of Cancer

Havana
Cuba

Pico Duarte
(10,417ft.)

San Juan

Puerto Rico

Guadeloupe

Dominica

St. Lucia

Jamaica   Hispaniola

Kingston

Port of Spain

Trinidad and Tobago

Venezuela

Caribbean Sea

Colombia

The World

A big map of the West Indies
and a small map of the world

4

Dear Duncan,

We are sailing around the West Indies. They are a long chain of **islands**. You can see the West Indies in red on the small map. They are between North America and South America.

Love,

Jane

P.S. Dad says that the islands of the West Indies stretch for 2,000 miles. If you stuck all the islands together to make one big island, it would be smaller than Oregon.

A black sandy beach in Dominica

Dear Denise,

The weather here is hot and wet. The West Indies are **tropical** islands. Sometimes there is a very strong wind, called a **hurricane**. It can do a lot of damage.

Love,

Clare

P.S. Mom says that the black sand on some beaches is from **volcanoes**. They were once under the sea. When they **erupted**, they made some of the islands in the West Indies.

A cruise ship stops at St. Lucia

Dear Penny,

Our ship is visiting some of the islands. Most of the people on the ship are on a vacation **cruise**. We stop at a new island every day. The islands are all different.

Love,

Michael

P.S. We travel around the islands by bus. I like to hear the people talking. On some islands, they speak English. On other islands, they speak Spanish, French, or Dutch.

Selling fruit at the market

Dear Andy,

We love to visit the food markets. There are all kinds of tropical fruits for sale. There are coconuts, bananas, mangoes, and limes. They all grow on these islands.

Your friend,

William

P.S. Mom likes to drink sugarcane juice. We drink all the time here because it is so hot. People like to eat meat with rice. They cook with hot chili peppers to add flavor.

A beach in the Bahamas

Dear Lenny,

We spent today on this beach. There are 700 islands in the Bahamas. The **capital** city is called Nassau. It is on the biggest island, which is called New Providence.

See you soon,

Janine

P.S. Dad says that Great Britain used to rule the Bahamas and the islands of Bermuda. That is why most of the people who live there speak English.

People dancing in Havana, Cuba

Dear Amy,

We are staying here in Havana. It is the capital city of the island of Cuba. We love the music here. It has a great beat. People dance to it in the streets.

Love,

Fran

P.S. Mom says that Spain ruled Cuba for 400 years. That is why most of the people here speak Spanish. Mom gave me some Cuban money, called *pesos*, to spend.

Dunns River waterfalls in Jamaica

Dear Jordan,

We flew to Jamaica. We landed at Kingston, which is the main town. We came to see these big waterfalls. Some people were climbing up them.

Love,

Alex

P.S. Mom thinks the beaches are lovely. There are lots of palm trees and mango trees. I used some money, called Jamaican dollars, to buy this postcard.

A hummingbird from the West Indies

Dear Isabel,

We have seen many beautiful birds here. I like the parrots and the hummingbirds best. We also saw some crocodiles. There are huge spiders here, too. They are called tarantulas.

Your friend,

Jim

P.S. The birds and animals live in a special park in Hispaniola. It is called a national park. The wildlife here is **protected**.

The fort of Castillo del Morro,
Puerto Rico

Dear Jodie,

Here in Puerto Rico, you pay for things with American money. There are lots of other American visitors. We have seen **factories**, stores, and some beautiful beaches, too.

Your friend,

Dale

P.S. The capital city of Puerto Rico is San Juan. Long ago, the fort called Castillo del Morro protected the city.

Fishing boats on a beach in Guadeloupe

Dear Paul,

We are heading south. This is the island of Gaudeloupe. A fisherman took us for a ride in his boat. We saw lots of fish. They were all different colors. We went swimming, too.

Love,

Anne

P.S. Dad says that France rules the island of Guadeloupe. Most of the people here speak French. Mom likes that because she can speak French, too.

Playing cricket

Dear David,

This is the place for sports. I knew that the West Indians were good at cricket. Their cricket teams play all over the world. They love soccer and **athletics**, too.

Love,

Shirley

P.S. Dad says that the West Indies send their teams to the **Olympic Games**. They win many medals for athletic events.

Children dressed up for the carnival in Trinidad

Dear Tom,

This is the island of Trinidad. There is a great **carnival** here. It happens in Port of Spain. There is a big procession. People dress up and dance in the streets.

Love,

Clive

P.S. My friend Jos lives on the island of Tobago. Everyone here dresses up at carnival time. Jos says that the music is the best part of all. He plays steel drums in a steel band.

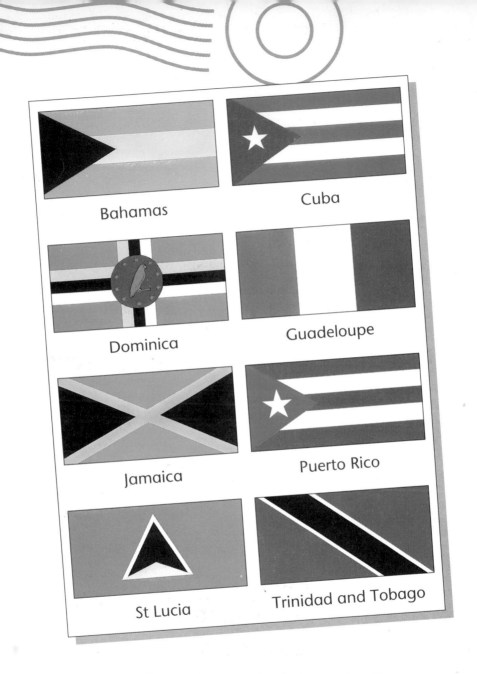

Bahamas

Cuba

Dominica

Guadeloupe

Jamaica

Puerto Rico

St Lucia

Trinidad and Tobago

Some flags from the West Indies

Dear Jack,

The islands all have their own flags. Some islands are still ruled by other countries. Today, the people on most of the islands choose their own rulers.

See you soon,

Marco

P.S. Mom says that when people choose their own rulers, the country is called a **democracy**. If a country has no king or queen, it is called a republic.

Glossary

Athletics: Sports such as running and jumping

Capital: The town or city where people who rule the country meet

Carnival: A time when people remember something that happened in the past. Some people wear special costumes.

Cruise: A vacation where you stay on a ship. The ship takes you to visit different places.

Democracy: A country where all the people choose the leaders they want to rule the country

Erupt: To throw out, or explode, with great force

Factory: A building where things are made

Hurricane: A storm with strong winds. It can cause a lot of damage.

Island: A piece of land with water all around it

National park: A park that belongs to the people of a country.

Olympic Games: An important world sports event. It takes place every four years.

Protected: Looked after. Wildlife is protected in national parks, so it will not die out.

P.S.: This stands for Post Script. A postscript is the part of a card or letter that is added at the end, after the person has signed it.

Tropical: Describes the hot, wet lands near the middle of the Earth. The heat from the sun is strongest here. We draw lines on maps to show the position of the tropics.

Volcanoes: Mountains made of rock from inside the Earth. The hot rock comes out through a hole at the top of a volcano.

Index